Dr Hugh Mungus was born. Prior to becoming a freelance sociologist, he was engaged for a time in animal husbandry, until he was caught. Over the years the doctor's incisive intellect and natural enthusiasm have led him to publish a number of learned studies, including *A Critical History of Gargling*, and to issue many profound philosophical observations, such as 'If a thing isn't worth doing, it isn't worth doing well', and 'He who hesitates is bossed'. Dr Mungus is perhaps best known for his 'Rules for Successful Living' ('If two wrongs don't make a right, try three'), and for his many inventions, among them the ground-to-air heat-seeking suppository.

Future enterprises include a study of ten terminal diseases that can be contracted on a crowded tube train, and completion of the long-awaited *Pop-Up Book of Common Prayer*. A man who has accomplished more than most in his lifetime, Dr Mungus nevertheless admits that he would give his right arm to be ambidextrous.

Totally
Tasteless
Graffiti

Hugh Mungus

CORGI BOOKS

TOTALLY TASTELESS GRAFFITI

A CORGI BOOK 0 552 12622 5

First publication in Great Britain

PRINTING HISTORY
Corgi edition published 1985
Corgi edition reprinted 1985

Copyright © Hugh Mungus 1985

This book is set in 10/11 Baskerville

Corgi Books are published by
Transworld Publishers Ltd., Century
House, 61–63 Uxbridge Road, Ealing,
London W5 5SA, in Australia by
Transworld Publishers (Aust.) Pty. Ltd.,
26 Harley Crescent, Condell Park, NSW
2200, and in New Zealand by
Transworld Publishers (N.Z.) Ltd., Cnr.
Moselle and Waipareira Avenues,
Henderson, Auckland.

Printed and bound in Great Britain by
Cox & Wyman Ltd, Reading

For Nettie,
last of the great
cuddlers

Totally
Tasteless
Graffiti

TOTALLY TASTELESS GRAFFITI

Psychologists have noted that sexual denial can lead to the development of bizarre sex fantasies. A lot of furtive, shaky-handed graffitists are clearly the products of that formula. Just as many, on the evidence of their cynical scratchings, appear to have been shaped by easy access to almost everything. A third group are guerrilla intellectuals, eager to disseminate their witty and incisive aphorisms via the classless medium of the wall-scrawl.

This collection concentrates on the work of a fourth category, people who show traces of the other three groups in their thinking, but whose candour and trenchant vulgarity set them distinctly apart. They're a bare-knuckled breed of scribblers with no time for even the outer limitations of good taste. Their blunt pencils often betray anger, which does wonders for their style, while a tenacious streak of humour redeems even the grosser specimens of their work.

5

I want to thank everybody who helped collect the material. Correspondents as far away as Los Angeles and Buffalo and as close to home as Welwyn and Barnsley have been tireless in gathering only the most pungently tasteless graffiti for inclusion here. In making the final selection, I have tried to adhere to the advice of the great John Osborne; 'Never break faith with bad taste.'

If this little book should cause offence or even outrage, I can't say I'll be surprised. I can't really say I'll be repentant, either.

Hugh Mungus

Down with vasectomy! Real men don't fire blanks.

BOLTON

I know a policeman who's so stupid, all the other coppers have noticed.

CELL WALL,
WEST LONDON
POLICE STATION

I'M NOT IN ANY ORGANISED
POLITICAL PARTY, I'M
A SOCIALIST.

REIGATE

If intellect was fusewire, you wouldn't find enough in here to go round a canary's cock.

STAFF ROOM,
COMPREHENSIVE
SCHOOL, DERBY

Danny La Rue wears men's clothes.

PUTNEY

Hypocrisy is the Vaseline of political intercourse.

Vimto is an anagram of vomit.

ADDED TO A
SOFT-DRINK
ADVERTISEMENT

Cliff Richard is covered in love bites – mostly self-inflicted.

The human brain is the only computer made of stuff like porridge.

OXFORD

Gynaecologists come in here to relax after a hard day at the orifice.

WINE-BAR WALL
NEAR ST STEPHEN'S
HOSPITAL,
FULHAM

KING KONG WAS A LESBIAN.

I love Brenda so much I can't shit.

Please help. I am blind.

WRITTEN ON A
CARD BY THE SIDE
OF A MAN BEGGING
IN SOUTHALL.
UNDERNEATH,
SOMEONE HAD
ADDED:

And he thinks he may be black

COPULATION IS SEX
BETWEEN CONSENTING
POLICE OFFICERS

EDINBURGH

I don't know exactly what Tampax is, but I want one. You can run with it, swim with it, play tennis with it, climb mountains . . .

YOUTH CLUB,
RUGBY

9

The great thing about screwing animals is they won't tell anybody.

WARWICK
UNIVERSITY

I, de Lord yo' God, got de big surprise fo' Enoch Powell.

FOLESHILL

Lorraine Chase has a room-temperature I.Q

Statistic: Cars hung with furry dice and other lucky charms always star in the really horrible accidents.

LAVATORY,
KENT PUB

Fuck faith and hope. Try greed and avarice instead. They always work.

ADDED TO A
BAPTIST CHURCH
POSTER,
MANCHESTER

Incoming traffic has the right of way.

GENTS,
LUTON

A young Bogside girl name of Alice
Took a leak in a Catholic chalice.
Said she, 'I did this
From a great need to piss,
And not from sectarian malice'.

BELFAST

Eat shit. Ten billion flies can't be wrong.

ON A REFECTORY
WALL AT ST
ANDREW'S
UNIVERSITY.
ADDED, IN
ANOTHER HAND:

Nor nine million Greeks, for that matter.

Oscar Wilde liked his vice versa.

God is a huge scarlet jelly bean.

ANGLICAN
COLLEGE

If you want to break a paddy's knuckles,
punch him in the nose.

BIRMINGHAM

You can always tell the Greenham Common
women by the curlers in their armpits.

HYDE PARK

When love has died and
the heart lies barren,
herpes lingers on.

GENTS,
PADDINGTON

An Egyptian virgin is any camel that can
run faster than an Arab.

BUS SHELTER,
GOLDERS GREEN

Love is a fellow feeling. Adultery is
another fellow feeling.

BEDFORD

12

There are two kinds of people in this world. Nice people and Protestants.

BALLYMENA

A smart engineer from Ascencion
Came up with a foreplay invention.
Its computerized lick
Gave his girlfriend a kick
But played hell with her
Pre-menstrual tension.

BRASENOSE
COLLEGE,
OXFORD

An alcoholic is any person who drinks more than his doctor.

PUB WALL,
GLASGOW

DON'T VOTE —
it only encourages
the bastards

AIDS: Anally
Injected
Death
Syndrome

LOS ANGELES

13

When the world has trodden and flattened you, when you're right down there on the floor, just get up, square your shoulders and yell, 'FUCK IT, I'M THROUGH!'

LAVATORY,
LONDON
ADVERTISING
AGENCY

Policemen wear numbers in case they get lost.

FULHAM PALACE
ROAD

TOM CATS ARE BALL-BEARING MOUSE TRAPS.

I crave some lip-lock on my love muscle.

LAVATORY,
USAF BASE,
MILDENHALL,
SUFFOLK

You're not really pissed if you can lie on the pavement without hanging on.

BERMONDSEY

What can you give a girl who has everybody?

GENTS,
LIVERPOOL

THE WAY TO
A WOMAN'S HEART
IS TO SAW HER
IN HALF.

READING

These toilets remind me of all the men I meet – they're either engaged or full of shit.

LADIES,
WARWICK

*There was a young rector of Kings
Whose mind was on heavenly things;
But his heart was on fire
For a boy in the choir,
Whose arse was like jelly on springs.*

CAMBRIDGE

*George's wife's had a revenge baby.
Some bastard had it in for George.*

The owner of this business is a coke-sacker.

OUTSIDE A SOLID
FUEL SUPPLY
DEPOT,
WARRINGTON

I thought an Itchifanni was a Japanese motorbike, until I discovered thermal underwear.

LADIES,
DEVON

Don't drink water.
Fish fuck in it.

TOTTENHAM

God ruined a perfect arsehole when he put a tongue in Tony Benn's mouth.

EUSTON

Everything except death is negotiable.

TUC BUILDING,
LONDON

Suicide is the sincerest form of self-criticism.

LONDON SCHOOL
OF ECONOMICS

Tomorrow is the last day of the best part of your life.

SIDMOUTH

Barbara Cartland has varicose brains.

PUBLIC LIBRARY,
LEAMINGTON SPA

At work, as in loving, you have to keep shoving.

CHEAPSIDE,
LONDON

Heroin isn't habit-forming. I should know, I've been taking it for years.

ADDICTION
CLINIC,
MANCHESTER

Onan was just a wanker.

GRAVESEND

Don't throw away unused condoms. They make great sleeping bags for white mice.

CONTRACEPTIVE
VENDING
MACHINE

Said a snuff-taking vicar, 'With ease,
I can stifle the noisiest sneeze'.
But in chapel one day
His arsehole gave way,
And shit filled his pants to the knees.

DUNDEE

Surgeons wear rubber gloves so they won't leave fingerprints.

GUY'S HOSPITAL,
LONDON

JR is using Sue Ellen as a crutch to lean on

CORBY

18

Oh, shit. I've stepped in some number two.

I'm a terrific lover. That's because I practise a lot on my own.

Tammy Wynette and Alice Cooper really know how hard it is to be a woman.

NICE GUYS FINISH LAST.

Don't order chicken in Italian restaurants. There's usually hair under the wings.

19

How did the Samba perform against the new Mercedes Sports? Just fine. Now try getting laid because you own one.

FELT-TIPPED ON
A TALBOT POSTER,
WIMBLEDON

BESIDE A DARK
PATCH ON A
URINAL WALL,
PITTSBURG:

Scratch 'n' sniff urine stain.

Never trust a faith-healer with contact lenses.

BARNET

I wouldn't trust MARK THATCHER as far as I could throw up.

Faint heart ne'er shafted a sheep.

LEEDS

20

My sister's so ugly, she has to put a bag over her head before her vibrator will work.

BATTERSEA

V.D. IS A GIFT THAT GOES ON GIVING.

GENTS.
BALHAM

Use Peter Pan Make-Up before your pan peters out.

POWDER ROOM.
CLARIDGES

Stevie Wonder doesn't wear sunglasses. Those are his nostrils.

WANDSWORTH

If Terry Wogan hadn't been invented, would it be necessary for him to exist?

TV CENTRE.
SHEPHERD'S BUSH

Jewish foreplay is fifteen minutes of pleading.

Said a thick-headed Greek called Anubis
I know all about pubes and boobies.
But I don't know the location
Of the bloody Eustachian,
Or where the fallopian tube is.

FACULTY OF
MEDICINE,
EDINBURGH
UNIVERSITY

Sudden prayers make GOD FART.

A P&O Cruise for a lasting Suntan.

TRAVEL AGENT'S
POSTER, TO WHICH
WAS ADDED:

A Reagan Cruise for an enduring radiation burn.

22

I wouldn't lead Jeremy Thorpe's life on a leash.

WESTMINSTER

The first Persian in Greece swam across. The rest walked over on the scum.

ALDERSHOT

If Ty-Phoo put the T in Britain, who put the cunt in Scunthorpe?

LINCOLN

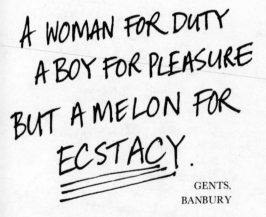

A WOMAN FOR DUTY
A BOY FOR PLEASURE
BUT A MELON FOR
ECSTACY.

GENTS,
BANBURY

If everything in life serves a useful purpose, how come Barry Manilow?

My I.U.D. picks up Radio Luxembourg

LEEDS
UNIVERSITY

I find Racial prejudice offensive.
I don't care for Polaks much, either.

NEW YORK

Communism will prevail and democracy
founder on the day Ray Charles hits a hole
in one.

AKRON,
OHIO

There was a young student of Oriel
Who flouted the ruling proctorial.
He ran down the Corn
With a huge throbbing horn
And buggered the Martyrs' Memorial.

MAGDALEN
COLLEGE,
OXFORD

*Fidel Castro does not eat shit sandwiches –
that is a vicious capitalist lie. Every well-
informed Marxist knows that he hates
bread.*

PAINTED ON A WALL
IN BRADFORD

'*If I lose my rag, they'll soon see how
things stand in India*'.

Mahatma Gandhi

*I want to join the Britt Ekland Youth
Opportunities Scheme.*

SCRIBBLED CARD
IN SOUTH
ENFIELD
JOB CENTRE

I LOST MY FIRST WIFE IN A WISHING WELL.

CATFORD

Russell Harty has a lot of class, most of it third.

WELWYN

Under the spreading chestnut tree
The village smith he sat,
Amusing himself
By abusing himself
And catching the load in his hat.

TECHNICAL
COLLEGE,
BURNBANK,
STRATHCLYDE

THE ONLY TIME MY WIFE AND I ARE SEXUALLY COMPATIBLE IS WHEN WE BOTH HAVE A HEADACHE!

Juan Miro paints pictures the way old people fuck.

COLORADO

The wages of sin vary a lot.

CAREFULLY INSCRIBED ON
A LAVATORY DOOR, CAMBRIDGE

'Neither a borrower nor a lender be.'

Shakespeare

ADDED BENEATH,
LESS CAREFULLY:

'Go and fuck yourself.'

D. H. Lawrence

A deaf leprechaun granted me a wish.
Now I've got a twelve-inch pianist.

PUB. DARTMOUTH

A theoretical physicist is like a eunuch in a
harem – he knows the lot, but there's
bugger all he can do about it.

ASTON
UNIVERSITY

SEX is DISGUSTING—
well it is the way
I do it ...   BANGOR

If God intended us to go metric, why did he give Jesus twelve disciples?

Abortion sucks

Kill a tree for Christmas

CARDIFF

YOU ARE WHAT YOU EAT

THE ABOVE. WRIT
LARGE ON A CARD
OUTSIDE A HEALTH
SHOP. ATTRACTED
THE COROLLARY:

YOU WERE WHAT YOU SHIT.

Please refrain from chewing the door handle while straining.

LAVATORY DOOR.
GLASGOW
UNIVERSITY

God broke the mould, then he made the Turks.

28

CHALKED ON THE WALL
IN FRONT OF AN
ABORTION CLINIC IN
SOUTH WARWICKSHIRE:

YOU RAPE 'EM, WE SCRAPE 'EM.

A Canadian lady, Anne Tunney,
Had a habit you may find quite funny;
She would roll up a buck
in her snatch ere she'd fuck,
So her husband could come into money

BOSTON,
MASS.

THE TEE-SHIRT BRAG
I'm six feet of dynamite

ATTRACTED THIS ADDITION,
WHILE THE WEARER WAS ASLEEP:

With a three-inch fuse.

LARRY THINKS HE'S
GETTING INSIDE MY
PANTS, BUT HE'S
WRONG. THERE'S ONE
ASS HOLE IN
THERE ALREADY.

LADIES,
NEBRASKA

BR SIGN:
*BICYCLES NOW TRAVEL FREE
ON BRITISH RAIL*

TO WHICH WAS ADDED:
*Irish cyclist knocked down by train at
Waterloo.*

A fool and his money are some party.

*Koo Stark used to be snow white.
But she drifted.*

SERVICE AREA, M1

*Minimize your problems. Think of crabs
as mobile dandruff.*

WASHROOM,
NHS CLINIC,
WEST LONDON

GO GAY — WIDEN THE
CIRCLE OF YOUR
FRIENDS

If it's moist, dry it; if it's dry, make it moist. Congratulations, you are now a dermatologist.

BLACKBOARD,
CLINICAL LECTURE
THEATRE,
EDINBURGH

Sex isn't everything.
It isn't plentiful for
a start.

It can't be a coincidence that 'banker' rhymes with 'wanker'.

WRITTEN IN NEAT
SCRIPT NEAR THE
DOOR OF NATWEST,
HOLBORN

I've a strong urge to return to the womb. Anybody's womb.

Midland culture is a contradiction in terms.

ARTS CENTRE,
WARWICK
UNIVERSITY

31

PENCILLED ON A STICKY
LABEL AFFIXED TO AN ESTATE
AGENT'S WINDOW:

*Come inside and sell your soul for a plot of
messuage.*

*If I want to attend a gay party, do I have
to be arsed first?*

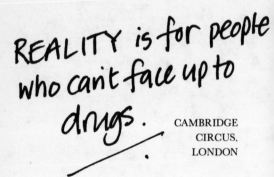

REALITY is for people
who can't face up to
drugs.

CAMBRIDGE
CIRCUS,
LONDON

University kills intellect by degrees.

I can see you reading this.

WRITTEN
ABOVE A TINY
HOLE IN THE
DOOR: LADIES
LAVATORY,
VICTORIA

There was a young scholar from Brighton
Who remarked to a tart, 'You're a tight
'un'.
She replied, 'Pon my soul,
You're in the wrong 'ole.
There's oodles of room in the right 'un'.

HULL
UNIVERSITY

**CHEMIST'S SIGN
AT DOVER:**

Sunglasses for the Continent.

**WITH THE FELT-PENNED
ADDITION:**

Rubber pants for the incontinent

**BY A DISPLAY OF
DEAD RABBITS OUTSIDE
A BERWICK STREET
BUTCHER'S SHOP:**

WATERSHIP DOWN:
You read the book!
You saw the film!!
Now – eat the characters!!!

THEY GIVE TERRIFIC
HEAD AT LEONARDS.

*The thinnest book in the world is called
'Great Irish Recipes'.*

*God may forgive you your carnal excesses,
but your mucous membranes won't.*

SALFORD

THE ONLY THING
IDENTICAL IN ALL
COUNTRIES IS THE
POLICE.

ESSEX
UNIVERSITY

Never get in a pissing fight with a skunk.

DENVER,
COLORADO

FACTORY SIGN:

WE HIRE THE HANDICAPPED

WITH ADDITION:

Two Poles work here.

My vibrator's the only slot machine I'm interested in.

LADIES,
YORK

Is Jesus divine – or is he just marvellous?

GAY BAR

I'm not afraid to call a spade a fucking shovel.

BUILDING SITE
OFFICE, HAYES

Nobody wants a faggot when he's fifty.

MEN'S ROOM,
LUNT'S THEATRE,
NEW YORK

PLATO WAS AC-BC

Jean Genet didn't write literature. He finger-painted in his own excrement.

BRIGHTON

35

My sister got her mink the way minks get minks.

LADIES,
KNIGHTSBRIDGE

David Attenborough has an obsession about slithery things fucking each other.

TOWCESTER

A gentleman is a guy who takes the dishes out of the sink before he pisses.

LADIES,
PURLEY

Roger Moore is a heterosexual.

These bogs are full of queers, flashers and degenerates. When somebody comes in for a straight shit, it's like a breath of fresh air.

GENTS,
TEDDINGTON

I can tell when Jane Fonda is menstruating.

BRENTFORD

Schweitzer was very stimulating on the organ.

LANGHAM
PLACE

Uranium and pussy are the two most dangerous things in the world.

BATH

HAEMORRHOIDS ARE THE REAL GRAPES OF WRATH.

A mathematician called Rex
Devised an equation for sex.
He proved a good fuck
Isn't patience or luck,
But a function of y over x.

EXETER
UNIVERSITY

FREE RUDOLPH HESS—
with every packet of shredded wheat.

BINGLEY

God isn't dead. He just won't come to the phone.

Reality is a fuck-up.

BUS STOP,
DONCASTER

There will be no more fighting in our streets. We just washed some Catholics and found out they're white.

DERRY

What choir sings only once a month? The Black and White Menstruals.

PLAYGROUND
WALL, HULL

The difference between an Ethiopian whore and an Ethiopian public toilet is that the toilet has a smaller hole – and it doesn't smell so bad.

BAR,
MICHIGAN

God is folding money.

COLNE

ON THE WALL OF
A HIGH SCHOOL
IN HARLEM:

ADVICE TO TEENAGERS
Use lots of drugs, anything you can lay hands on, because soon your body won't be able to handle that punishment, and all you'll be able to do is drink.

One in the hand is nothing like two in the bush.

MARGATE

Diana Ross is Michael Jackson in drag.

ROTHERHAM

Sir Robin Day is no longer beneath my contempt.

PALMER'S
GREEN

Too many cocks spoil the brothel.

The Ayatollah Khomeinei is a bigger bum than two arses.

HYDE PARK

A fussy young lass called McEwan
Disliked the idea of screwin'.
'I finger my muffin,
It's safer than stuffin',
And besides I can see what I'm doin'.'

HARROW

The public is a
WHORE !

DETROIT

CELIBACY IS A NOCTURNAL OMISSION

KEBLE
COLLEGE,
OXFORD

*Paranoia has gone all the way to the top.
God thinks He's Margaret Thatcher.*

BLACKBURN

*Turds taper so that the buttocks won't
come together with a slap.*

GENTS,
PUTNEY

*You know you're getting middle-aged when
your friends' children start making you feel
horny.*

BOSTON,
MASS.

7 MILLION GUINNESS ARE DRUNK EVERY DAY

BEER MAT,
WITH THE
BALLPOINT
COMMENT:

I'd no idea there were so many piss-artists in the family

Jerzy Kosinski is the six-foot Pole I wouldn't touch anybody with.

PORTLAND,
OREGON

It takes eleven hundred neon tetras to make a sandwich.

PET SHOP,
LONDON SW

LET YOUR FINGERS DO THE WHACKING.

GENTS,
WITNEY

Where would Christianity be if Jesus had pulled eight to fifteen with time off for good behaviour?

EVANSTON,
ILLINOIS

AN ERECTION HAS NO CONSCIENCE.

There was a young fellow from Thrale,
Who wasn't exactly male;
His drive wasn't channelized
So he got psycho-analysed,
And now he can't get enough tail.

BASINGSTOKE

A rat is a sturdy, healthy mammal that develops cancer the second it enters a laboratory.

VETERINARY
COLLEGE,
GLASGOW

If Ralph Nader had a penis as big as his mouth, his immortality would be guaranteed.

SEATTLE
WASHINGTON

SEMEN IS FATTENING

*God is a convergence of events leading to a
sales opportunity.*

*Men seldom make passes at girls with thin
arses.*

*I tried powdered rhino horn. Now every
time I get an erection, I charge Land
Rovers.*

*If you want your dog to learn how to beg,
let it into our bedroom.*

How do we know Jesus was Jewish? Well, he was 33, unmarried, and his mother thought he was God.

DANBURY,
CONNECTICUT

I thought clap was a form of applause until I discovered Soho.

Suicide tip: stand next to a Cypriot and inhale.

LONDON

The thinnest book in the world is called 'Great Jewish Boxers.'

There's no such thing as a mild heart attack.

CASUALTY
DEPARTMENT

A man should be greater than some of his parts.

CARDIFF

An erotic neurotic called Sid
Got his Ego snarled up with his Id.
His errant libido
Was like a torpedo
And that's why he done what he did.

HEREFORD

Wear two at a time—
TO BE SURE, TO BE SURE

CONTRACEPTIVE
VENDING
MACHINE,
BELFAST

Cindy's snatch is a clap trap.

PORTLAND,
OREGON

LAVATORY SIGN:
NOW WASH YOUR HANDS

WITH ADDITION:
*YOU KNOW WHERE THEY'VE
BEEN*

*I want a woman with a healthy body and a
sick mind.*

46

If God hadn't intended man to eat pussy, he would't have made it look like taco.

SACRAMENTO,
CALIFORNIA

A penis is the only thing that has to be grown before it can be planted.

GENTS,
MIDDLETON

*Gay: Got
     Aids
     Yet?*

LOS ANGELES

If you wrap Sellotape round hamsters, they won't split when you fuck them.

LINCOLN

VASECTOMY CUTS OFF YOUR HEIR SUPPLY.

SHEFFIELD

In engineering terms, a woman is poorly designed – the intake is far too near the exhaust.

BRADFORD
UNIVERSITY

Charles Bronson's got muscles in his piss.

CHICAGO

GET THE ABBEY HABIT-
SHACK UP WITH A MONK

Have you tried Andrew's?
– Everybody has.

WINDSOR PUB

Scots Protestants are more bigoted than Scots Catholics, because it's easier to say 'Fuck the Pope' than it is to say 'Fuck the Moderator of the General Assembly of the Church of Scotland'.

SAUCHIEHALL
STREET,
GLASGOW

A fart is the sharpest thing in nature. It can go through your trousers without making a hole.

GENTS,
PITLOCHRY

Ronnie Corbett has to roll down his socks to pee.

BLACKPOOL

IS MUFFIN THE MULE A PERVERSION?

Sir Keith Joseph is either crazy or both.

LONDON

The Pill is a bedroom sweet with a less-fattening centre.

ON A NOTICE
IN A FAMILY
PLANNING
CLINIC

Ignorance is power.

Je suis car je ponce.

SOHO

RONALD REAGAN
IS BILINGUAL. HE SPEAK
ENGLISH AND BULLSHIT.

ORPINGTON

*If I owned Barnsley and a sewage farm,
I'd rent out Barnsley and live in the
sewage.*

YORK

*The trouble with women is they've always
got something up with their wedding
tackle.*

GENTS,
SHOREDITCH

*I'd like to meet Philip Roth, but I
wouldn't want to shake his hand.*

LAWRENCE,
MASS.

Fuck mental health!

I respect my wife's body, I regard it as a temple – it's somewhere to go on Sunday morning.

GENTS,
CRAWLEY

WRITTEN IN A
CULTIVATED
HAND ON A
NOTICE BOARD
AT A CHURCH
YOUTH CLUB:

Always be nice to people. Especially underprivileged children. Take every opportunity to help, and remember kindness and compassion are a balm for the wounded spirit. On the other hand don't take no shit off nobody.

Mother Theresa

Its better to eat noodles than Jewish girls — noodles wriggle

KIRKSVILLE,
MISSOURI

SHOWER-DOOR BOAST:
I'm seven inches long and an inch in diameter.

TO WHICH WAS APPENDED:
Amazing. What size is your prick?

Aberdonians are living proof that the Celts fucked cattle.

BERWICK

God's embrace is wide, encompassing the spectrum of faith and being. He loves all Catholics, all Protestants, each Hindu, every Muslim, and the occasional Hebrew.

TUFFNELL
PARK

Semen and urine look different, so that Irishmen can tell whether they're coming or going.

COVENTRY

*My sister's a better screw than my mother.
– She knows. Your father told her.*

GENTS,
HIGHBURY

I know the Dean doesn't fuck poodles – but
I want to hear him deny it in public.

CAMPUS
WALL,
CALIFORNIA

I WAS A GAY
NECROPHILIAC, TILL
SOME ROTTEN ASSHOLE
SPLIT ON ME

FLORIDA

IN A MUSIC
PUBLISHER'S WASHROOM:
I learned the truth at seventeen,
A girl must keep her privates clean;
Well, if you want the truth!

Janis Ian

Some say cocaine makes girls frisky,
But I think whisky's less risky.

KING'S ROAD
BOUTIQUE

Equality means he sleeps on the clammy patch.

Arrange the following words into a well-known phrase or saying: OFF FUCK.

USE MAX FACTOR'S KNACKER LACQUER — IT ADDS LUSTRE TO YOUR CLUSTER

*The dick of a fellow named Randall
Fired sparks like a big Roman candle;
He was much in demand,
For the colours were grand,
But his wife found him too hot to handle.*

Swallow a spoonful of shit first thing in the morning and nothing worse will happen to you all day.

Some girls are born great, others have greatness thrust into them.

SUSSEX

**BY AN EMPTY
TOILET PAPER
DISPENSER:**

*DO NOT LINGER—
USE YOUR FINGER.*

I asked for Gloria Vanderbilt's autograph and she signed my ass.

NEW YORK

Masturbation is the thinking man's television.

God saw the mess snails leave behind, so he gave women legs.

RAIN
SHELTER,
YARMOUTH

Jesus saves.
— He'll have a lot more credibility when he
invests.

STAMFORD

I'm so old, I remember DORIS DAY before she became a Virgin.

Slip an ice lolly in one of these and give her
a deep freeze for Christmas.

CONTRACEPTIVE
MACHINE

FELT-TIPPED BY
THE NAPKIN DISPOSAL
BAGS ON A COVENTRY
LADIES:

PACK A LUNCH FOR A
VAMPIRE

I thought Wan King was a place in China,
until I went blind.

KENILWORTH

I don't mind having a test-tube baby,
providing it's an eight-inch test tube.

Lose weight without dieting. Pick your
nose regularly.

HIGHBURY

ON A WALL, LAMBETH:

YOU CAN'T BUY JUSTICE IN
BRITAIN!

AND CHALKED UNDERNEATH:
No, but you can certainly rent it.

MOTHER THERESA
WAS A BUNNY GIRL.

IPSWICH

What's blue and fucks old ladies?
– Hypothermia.

LEAMINGTON
SPA

Dr Spooner would call Arthur Scargill a shining wit.

LEEDS

Macho is a guy who stands up to shit.

MIAMI

The three commonest lies in the world:
a) Of course I love you.
b) The cheque's in the post.
c) I promise not to come in your mouth.

NORTH
KENSINGTON

Try the new 'Boycott' curry. You still get the runs, but very slowly.

HUDDERSFIELD

WRITTEN ON THE
FLYLEAF OF A GIDEON
BIBLE:

And God rebuked Eve, saying, Thou should'st not have bathed in the river. How shall I ever get that smell off the fish?

58

Should priests be allowed to marry?
– Only if they really love each other.

LIVERPOOL

The definition of 'Gaelic' is one Irish poof
going down on another Irish poof.

WARDOUR
STREET,
LONDON

Santa comes but once a year – and down a
chimney, at that.

BELFAST

Adrenalin is brown.

COMBAT
SCHOOL,
ALDERSHOT

Commie condoms are red riding hoods.

ORPINGTON

Telly Savalas has more hair than talent.

NEW YORK

I'm too Jung to be a Freud.

OXFORD

Only toothless fairies can go to goblin parties.

Women come and go, but your mates are here forever.

TENEMENT WALL, BIRMINGHAM

CHINESE SEDUCTION
Hand in hand;
Hand in gland;
Gland in gland;
Gland!

WARWICK UNIVERSITY

Q: What's black and full of holes?
A: Marvin Gaye.

I never wore rubber underpants until I discovered Tennent's Lager.

PAINTED ON A WALL IN DERRY:

Dr Paisley is the mouthpiece of decency and sanity in this province!

TO WHICH WAS ADDED:

How is it possible to be a mouthpiece and an arsehole simultaneously?

Reagan's so full of
shit, his eyes are
brown.

OUR BETTY'S HAD MORE PRICKS THAN A SECOND-HAND DART BOARD

God bless the wound that never heals,
The harder you stroke it, the softer it feels.
You can wash it with soap, you can scrub it
in soda,
But nothing gets rid of the John West
odour.

LITTLE
RISSINGTON

What do you call a man with a rabbit up
his arse?
– Warren.

GENTS,
BRISTOL

Q: What's got 200 balls and fucks
rabbits?
A: A shotgun.

UPWEY,
DORSET

Is a fluorescent turd just a flash in the pan?

GENTS,
TAMWORTH

The only part of Popeye that doesn't rust is the part he puts in Olive Oil.

FLORIDA

Betty ****'s got Parrot's Disease – she's had a cock or two.

EAST
KIRKBY,
YORKSHIRE

The Lord made creatures, large and small,
Some that slither, some that crawl;
Broadcasting House employs them all.

WASHROOM,
LANGHAM
GALLERY,
LONDON

DO BLIND PEOPLE
GO ON DEAF DATES?

Holy Virgin, we believe
That, sinless, thou didst yet conceive.
Blessed Mother, thus believing,
May we sin without conceiving?

LADIES,
HULL
UNIVERSITY

OK, I admit it, I'm paranoid – but it's
only because the whole fucking world's out
to get me.

HARVARD

What do you call a Welshman with a stick
up his arse?
– Taffy Apple.

To the Virgins of
Edinburgh — thanks
for nothing.

PRINCES ST

Russell Grant thinks he's pregnant because
his piles stopped bleeding.

FULHAM

Hell hath no fury like a woman spermed.

NO EASTER THIS YEAR.
The body's turned up.

All this hassle about the Government's homosexuality bill - why don't they just pay the bloody thing?

MARBLE ARCH

I admire feminists - especially the ones with big tits and nicely rounded arses.

DUNSTABLE

IRATE GRAFFITO
ON A TEMPERAMENTAL
COFFEE MACHINE, LEEDS:

There's more chance of screwing Kate Bush than there is of getting a drink from this bleeding thing.

JOHN LENNON LIVES!
– Oh shit, really? They've gone and buried him!

HAMMERSMITH

Q: What's the difference between a cricket bat and a guinea pig?
A: You can't fuck a cricket bat.

Annie Sugden cheats on the housekeeping.

BRADFORD

William Faulkner is alive and drunk in New Orleans.

LOS ANGELES

SYPHILIS
IS A SORE POINT

You'll never get pregnant while you're in a lousy job that pays peanuts.

LADIES
RICHMOND

Reasonable people accomplish fuck all.
                    CROYDON

MAKE LOVE NOT WAR,
NOBODY EVER GOT
KILLED BY A TIT.

ON A LANDSCAPERS' SITE HUT,
WITH AN ARROW POINTING TO
A PILE OF CUT TURF:

GREEN SIDE UP, PADDY.

It's always darkest before the lights go out.

*Q: What do you get when you cross a pussy
with a computer?
A: A cunt that knows everything.*

AIRDRIE,
STRATHCLYDE

It's always a pleasure at Hank's
To go for a stroll on the banks.
One time in the grass
I stepped on an ass,
And heard a young girl murmur,
'Thanks.'

TOWSON,
MARYLAND

You could wade through the depths of
Margaret Thatcher's charity without wet-
ting your ankles.

BLACKPOOL

What's the difference between hot water
and Des O'Connor?
– Hot water bucks up the feet.

UPMINSTER

NOTHING SUCCEEDS
LIKE A BUDGIE
WITH NO BEAK.

LYMINGTON

All I want is a girl somewhere,
Made of teak like a sturdy chair,
With well-carved hips and hair,
Oh, wooded tit be loverly!

                                        Pinocchio

OEDIPUS WAS A REAL MOTHERFUCKER.

RADIATION FADES YOUR GENES.

                                        SOUTH
                                        LONDON

ON A GARAGE WORKSHOP,
BRIGHTON:
Good news for Marc Bolan fans –
we've got the mini back on the road.

Cunnilingus is a matter of taste.

                                        SOUTHALL

Write your own Graffiti . . .

Write your own Graffiti . . .

Write your own Graffiti . . .

Write your own Graffiti . . .

Write your own Graffiti . . .

OTHER HUMOROUS TITLES AVAILABLE FROM CORGI/BANTAM BOOKS

WHILE EVERY EFFORT IS MADE TO KEEP PRICES LOW, IT IS SOMETIMES NECESSARY TO INCREASE PRICES AT SHORT NOTICE. CORGI BOOKS RESERVE THE RIGHT TO SHOW AND CHARGE NEW RETAIL PRICES ON COVERS WHICH MAY DIFFER FROM THOSE ADVERTISED IN THE TEXT OR ELSEWHERE.

THE PRICES SHOWN BELOW WERE CORRECT AT THE TIME OF GOING TO PRESS

☐	99052 3	Cynics Dictionary	Russell Ash	£2.50
☐	12272 6	Dame Edna's Bedside Companion (Large Format)	Dame Edna Everage	£3.95
☐	12624 1	The Little Black Book	J. J. Gabay	£1.50
☐	99053 1	Out of Order	Frank Johnson	£2.50
☐	98079 X	Graffiti: The Scrawl of the Wild	Roger Kilroy	£1.50
☐	98116 8	Graffiti 2	Roger Kilroy	£1.50
☐	11812 5	Graffiti 3	Roger Kilroy	£1.25
☐	99022 1	Graffiti 4	Roger Kilroy	£1.50
☐	99045 0	Graffiti 5: As the Actress Said to the Bishop	Roger Kilroy	£1.50
☐	11913 X	Illuminated Limericks	Roger Kilroy	£1.25
☐	12622 5	Totally Tasteless Graffiti	Hugh Mungus	£1.50
☐	12436 2	The Book of Narrow Escapes	Peter Mason	£1.50
☐	12681 0	It's Different in the Country	Liz Potter	£1.75
☐	12399 4	Any Fool Can Be A Pig Farmer	James Robertson	£1.75
☐	12532 6	Hooray For Yiddish	Leo Rosten	£3.95
☐	12258 0	The Book of World Sexual Records	G. L. Simons	£1.95
☐	12402 8	Fanny Peculiar	Keith Waterhouse	£1.95
☐	22919 2	Last Official Sex Maniacs Joke Book	Larry Wilde	£1.50

All these books are available at your bookshop or newsagent, or can be ordered direct from the publisher. Just tick the titles you want and fill in the form below.

CORGI BOOKS, Cash Sales Department, P.O Box 11, Falmouth, Cornwall.

Please send cheque or postal order, no currency.

Please allow cost of book(s) plus the following for postage and packing:

U.K. CUSTOMERS – Allow 55p for the first book, 22p for the second book and 14p for each additional book ordered, to a maximum charge of £1.75.

B.F.P.O. & EIRE – Allow 55p for the first book, 22p for the second book plus 14p per copy for the next seven books, thereafter 8p per book.

OVERSEAS CUSTOMERS – Allow £1.00 for the first book and 25p per copy for each additional book.

NAME (Block Letters) ....

ADDRESS ....

....